The Eloquence Series

The Love I Feel For You

This work is dedicated to the one that I loved more than life itself. I have always loved you, and sadly I probably always will love you. However, I wonder if you ever loved? If you did not then it is best that you did leave. Yet, you should have stayed around to see how much I loved you, to understand what I was truly feeling for you. I am sorry that you never found out how much I loved you.

Contents

Devotion

I can't be your friend, cause I couldn't see you with another.

I can be your man but I rather be your lover.

If you can't be with me, then I will have none other.

I will cherish, care and love you better than any brother.

I will be only with you, until the Pastor puts us under.

If you go before I do, my heart will have no other.

The Love I Feel For You

...

I loved you and it hurts to say that I still do.

I loved only two men in my life exclusive of God and Jesus Christ.

You and my father

You I loved more than any man that I have ever desired.

I saw a future, a present, and no past or end in sight

for the love that I feel and felt for you existed even beyond this

life.

For you, I would've gone happily into the eternal darkness and

unknown and waited patiently

Patiently waited for your arrival in Heaven, and looked for you

again – endlessly - in the next life.

For you were my world

and my love

and nothing you desired would've been out my reach to build the

life and existence that I wanted

for us.

For the love that I feel for you

and felt for you

would have only consumed me and made me wait

patiently,

and eternally,

...

for only a kiss from you in this life

and the next.

Endlessly I have loved ... you

To what end haven't I loved you?

Showed you. Told you.

Showered you with gifts, love, and affection.

Only to be shown nothing but rejection.

I ran to you at the end of each day to see you;

Hear your laughter and wonder about you at night.

I try to kiss you

Only for you to push me away even with no one in sight.

I tell you that I love so you need not wonder ...

So that you will know.

Only to see that I can't get pass your door.

I hope for the chance or the day that you would respond in kind.

Yet it is a figment of my imagination

As you leave me hanging each time.

Each night as I drop you off I know that you are pulling away.

Each night even this night

Wishing you were by my side

Knowing that you will never stay.

I hide the pain with my tears wishing you would open up to me.

Never thinking that the problem might just be me.

I wonder what should I ask for as I lay and pray.

Knowing you will never love me even to your dying day.

I would've loved you until

I became...

The man you should've love

The man you desired

The man of your dreams

The nigga of your nightmares

The lover of your soul

Your future yet untold

The guy that lusted for you

Who saw you all to true

The man who would be a partner

The one you would've fought for

The guys whose heart you would capture

with only a look of your rapture

The man who fell for you

That I would only be true

This is the man I would be

Yet ... you'll never see

Aint' I a woman too?

Don't my breast heave and my back arch?

Cain't I put my hands on my hips

     and let my backbone slip

        elude sexuality/sensuality

Why does my sexuality have to play a part?

Ain't I a woman, too

Cain't I be me, free

fine, genuine

divine baby

Cain't I be a woman?

  The woman

Are my mounds to fine,

     round

     perked

     perplexed

     jolting?

Cain't I learn from my sisters and from wince I came

Cain't I look at that moon and let it guide my way

Lean on my sisters for strength and support

The patriarchs no longer hold us

We understand our heritage

Don't we have a fervent spirit for righteousness?

      Holding our heads high and inspiring others

Ain't I a woman too?

Cain't I be a woman, too?

Arrival of a Missed lover

winds blow

pheromones released

a lover arrives

a desire of want

quick knowing looks

eyes aflutter

passion of a touch

a kiss exchanged

pecks on the cheek

a touch of the lips

soft caresses

tongues dueling

heavy breathing

turns taken

a need fulfilled

sublime bliss

Beauty Within Us All

You are beautiful

You are black

I have beauty

We are strong!

Words to empower myself do not come easy

    but it comes when my heart is wounded and

    my soul is in jeopardy

We are lively, soulful, colorful beings that

    pull ourselves up by our apron strings

As blacks we are a forgiving community

We embrace our brothers or sisters in various

    aspects of their life

We are acknowledging

Spiritual, lovely, religious, brilliant

Oppressed (but singin' a hymn from our souls)

(No apologies)

Accepting

Tooth suckin', lips smackin', finger snappin',

    hands movin', vogue-in youths

I am harsh

I am cold

angry but real

worshipping but unworshipped

unwanted not wanting but wanting

needing but to high and saditty to acknowledge the need

    to need others

Gifted shamans,

artistic

Innovative

tasteful

we are all that-we know not why, but we are

Eternal guilt, hearts as big as wells

I am butch

I am femme

I am human

I am a person

I am BLACK?!?

I am damn proud

We are loved

I am liked

We have brothers (embrace them)

Disgrace is not an option

Have your surgery my brother and become my sistah

Love your mate

Hit his ass when he has done wrong?

    but pull him to you and forgive him?

Love him and

Live your life, but live YOUR life with or without him.

Wearing of Masks

sit up straight

act "normal"

read that person

inject that thought

ask him how he doing

oh, that was a joke, laugh

HA HA HA...

yes your thoughts are ragin',

but you will be fine

don't think about what you have become

don't cry baby!

back to being "normal"

"fine"

"Oh, I am fine, and how are you doing?"

head up

chin out

walk with dignity

go to class, study

see frat, grip him up

show assertiveness

naw he does not know about...

"the incident"

laugh at his joke

no, don't sit in the dark crying

work harder, study harder

occupy your mind

don't deal with it

it will work itself out

call a friend

laugh, joke, smile

don't cry baby

"Act like Kirk Yancy Williams!"

outgoing, voiceful, very FIERCE

cute, cuddly, romantic, supportive

read him

"No I am not crying, I am just watering my goatee."

don't dance and listen to music

to release the tension

you are not restless,

do not toss and turn in your sleep

"the incident" is over

laugh at it baby, laugh at it!

it is all in your mind.

It is all in your mind!

IT IS ALL IN YOUR MIND!!!

hold me baby.

He greeted me at the bus terminal--no kiss!?! I hadn't seen him in days, but it felt like ages. The sexual tension and attraction had mounted, and it was evident.

I gave him a lingering hug and a quick peck on the right side of his neck. I let go, but I needed another hug. I looked him in his eyes, and he was as handsome as ever.

He took my bag and walked with me as I walked to the counter to purchase my ticket for my connecting ride home. We shared our life experiences from the previous days as we walked to the gate and while I waited in line. I noticed that the tension began to build. As he spoke, I interrupted him with the occasional, "Ba' .... Damn I love you," and "I miss you... with your fine ass." He blushed, his eyes lite, and he responded with, "I missed you too...," and "I love you too."

We began touching each other's chest and body unconsciously. Damn the tension was building. He is F-I-O-N-E.

It was time to go. He gave me my bag back, and we hugged a long lingering hug. I looked into his eyes and we kissed. Smack on the lips. Sweet and soft.

I needed another, so I took it. Right there in the long crowded line.

"Call me." He walked away.

I looked over and I saw her lips turned up and eyes wide with shock. "Get use to it baby. You flaunt your sexuality in public, and I will flaunt that kiss. I do not want you, I want him."

It was the first time I kissed him in public, and I will do it again.

May 20th, 199-

Reflections on April 20th

To my "Panamanian Lover"

It was a month ago that I took you into my arms and I have not regretted it thus far. You have become a part of me that I want to keep for some time. You might think I stole your heart, but you were stealing mine just as much as I was stealing yours. I think about you, what you mean to me, and I smile because you have a place in my heart. Your spirit and personality is causing mine to rejoice, jump, and it wants to embrace yours. Now that I see that our spirits are compatible, I wonder if our souls will mate.

It has been a month now that you slept in my arms and my bed. I need to feel you in that way again. When you were here, I felt rejuvenated, and at peace. Since you left, I had some "emotional difficulties," but when I think of you, things become better and I am happier.

Last night I slept at my lover's house. Yes I slept in his bed, but I could not sleep because I was wishing it was you that was near me instead of him.

It was a month ago that I felt this passionate about someone, and again I feel this way about you. The feelings that I felt for you a month ago were so intense, so instinctive that it surprised me, and still surprises me. You see Antonio, it was then that I opened my heart to you and I began to show you a side of me that no one sees so soon, or ever.

Antonio it was a month ago that I kissed you. When I kissed you, I did not want to stop, and this night, I want to kiss you again and not want to stop. When I stopped kissing you, and holding you, I felt empty. Tonight, let me not feel that way again. That night when I looked into your eyes, I knew I wanted you. I wanted you then and I want you now... boy do I want you now.

It was a month ago that I met you. Since then my life has changed, astonishingly.

Antonio, four weeks ago, you and I shared ourselves in a loving physical nature and since then I have been wanting you even more. It was a month ago that I, we felt the sweating of our efforts, and it is looked upon with the FONDEST of memories.

Baby it was a month ago that you felt the emotions that I expressed, and I have one question, can you feel it now?

You asked a question that I must answer. You know I love you. I love your mind, your personality, your humor, and your spirit. I love you emotionally, and physically. Even though you can not be here at times, you know where I want you. I want you in my heart, in my bed, in my thoughts, in my arms, in that space of my soul that only you fill.

I want you in my life and I want you by my side, always.

With the deepest affections,

Your Energizer Bunny

Promises and Expectations

I can't promise you anything!

Nothing but love

affection

emotion

honesty

and me.

I thought about you

and how I would like to spend time with you...

Holding you,

Lovin' you,

Caressin' you....

Making you feel like you the most special thing in my life.

And given time.....

You will be.

I wonder how you would react to know that I could lov... like you.

Like you with all my heart.

Yeah

You know what I mean...

The kind of like that makes me want to hold you all night
and whisper into your ear,
"Everything will be all right..."

That kind of like that makes me want to

cuddle up to ya'

hold ya' tight

caress your chest

and listen to our hearts beat

aaallllll   nnniggghhhtt   llllooonnnggggg......

UMPH!

And I thought about you today.

"cause I am black?"

Fuck that of me kickin yo' door in while you ain't there

sheeit, I want a challenge

I gonna visit your house when you are there...

perhaps while you are making love to your man

yeah I am into that voyeurism shit,

niggas love a threesome...

or perhaps I will kick the door down during your dinner party of

White Anglo-Saxon of European Decent friends and demand all

the cash, and slap a white bitch on the way out...

no, here is one better.

I *will* roll up to your crib, and *take* all your shit!

Let me tell you how I am gonna do it ...

While you are out at little Billy's baseball game

I am gonna send my boy "Slim" in through the doggy door

that you leave open for "Fluffy"

and we gonna take all you shit ...

TV, Blu-Ray, cable box, watches, rings,

even your monogram bath towels

that you put out on holidays,

(well not this Christmas)

I'll walk into your bedroom

and look through your drawers and find the evidence that you

are fucking your husband's best friend ...

"Oh this bitch is wild! She into that freaky shit,

my kind of freaky shit!"

Go into the kitchen and make myself a sandmich and drank yo'

Orange Juice

Fo' I roll, I'm gonna leave a note for your husband Billy

telling him how you fucking round on him

either that or I gonna blackmale yo' ass for money for my habit

Sisters, do not think I am not after you too...

Oh no, I am not gonna steal your purse.

That shit is old!

I gonna wait until we in a relationship and then I am gonna

milk you for all yo' shit!

Fuck up your credit, get credit cards in my name, cash your checks, get some wages, tips, fuck up savings, car and an extra copy of the house keys.

I hope you on welfare and medicare. I'll shave off this goatee and Mustache and act like little Jamal.

Go in there with your card and get my teethes fixed, eyes checked.

Soon as I get out...

Just five more days

Your misunderstanding of me

We, being black and uneducated

we know what it is like to sing the blues

We, being black and selfish,

know the anguish of hardship and the hatred for our brothers

Brothers that are unable to congratulate our brothers

for fear that we will be looked down upon

we don't

we, being black and poor

always looking for a hand out, hook ups, gifts, etc...

just give me a little piece

we, being lazy and shiftless

not knowing how to work and earn things cause,

we be lazy and trifling.

Your misunderstanding of me.

Longing for a lover

I want you here
like I have wanted no other man
I think about you and the way that we were
while you were here.
We talked, we laughed, we shared a part of our life that
neither of us wanted to end.
You took care of me, held me in your arms,
and gave me stability that no one ever gave
me.

I want a shoulder to cry on
a place to put my emotions
show my fears
give me affection
a place to cast all my sorrows and
my worries.
With you I have life, sanity, humanity
emotions
dignity

and pain.

I want you closer

so that we can share things like we

shared when you we here.

I want to see your smiling face in the morning

feel you near me like I always have

to wake up to you and having you kiss me

caress me

wake me in that old fashion way of letting me know

you are here with me.

I want to be held by YOU!

Again

like only you have held me

I remember you trying to kiss me

me licking my lips before every kiss

and you laughing.

I remember the security and the warmth

that I felt in your arms

the way that we cuddled on the sofa

and

read

got to know each other

and tickling me until I

laughed uncontrollably

I MISS YOU…

And everything we did together

going to class

dining together.

Showering and washing each other's body

The back rubs that caused a

plethora of emotion and memories

It's too damn lonely at night. All these dumb ass men

around and all I want is you.

I HAVE NEEDS!!!

And one of them is you.

Preferences

I like my men dark.

I never look at the physical features: smooth, short, with a tummy. Something to hold on to at night. Sensible ... intelligent, voiceful, emotional.

Wide hips, thick thighs, big lips, big gentle hands that when he rubs my body, they become lazy like. Nice big butt, the kind that you can set a saucer of milk on in the morning and come back in the afternoon and have butter. Long luscious legs, smooth skin, sexy voice, and nipples, kissable, suckable.

I love my baby. That way he thinks, the way he walks, the way he speaks. A deep baritone voice that goes deeper in the morning as we wake. His looks ... a cute boyish smile, with dimples to match. Eyes: light brown, and caring, sensitive, a window to his soul. A soul I know oh-so-well.

He has other nice features: a close-cut hair cut that allows me easy access to his head. I like the way he moans when I rub my fingers in his head, and when I scratch his scalp, wash his hair in the shower, and rub his head when I am just near him being playful.

His shoulders are wide, broad ... able for me to place my hands on them, feel his muscles under them. Big strong shoulders that lets me know that he can carry the weight of the world on them.

His chest is not very muscular ... don't get me wrong, it has definition. Medium build, with nice suckable nipples. I like his chest. I can place my head on it for comfort and support. I fall asleep on it at night while running my fingers over his abdomen.

His legs are smooth, hair-less, nice. Short, flexible, with strength, and muscularity. Strong, shapely, masculine!

Nice hips, that flows when he walks. He has a stride in his step that lets me know that he is a man, all man.

His skin is dark. A nice walnut color. It's also smooth. His lips are small, but full, volumptious, strong.... kissable, suckable.

He is caring, human, and affectionate. We have a lot of things in common in regards to what we are looking for in terms of feelings.

Our pasts are also very similar because we have had others interested for themselves and their own gain.

I like the way that he receives things from me. My best memory of his is at his home. We decided to have a romantic evening together. We turned down the lights, and relaxed on the couch. I placed his head in my lap, looked into his eyes ... kissed him, and began to feed him strawberries with whip cream. I cradled his head on my lap and ran my fingers through his hair.

He smiled, like a Cheshire cat. Glowing, beaming, eyes sparkling. Later he sang to me. A sweet song, "My Funny Valentine." We made love until the sun came up.

I like the way that he kiss my ears and licks behind them to hear me laugh.

The way that he nibbles on them. The way he sings, and his voice. It is romantic. I would never give that up, or jeopardize what we have. He is special, and unique. I love him for that.

Damn he is a Fuckable Cutie.

Acceptance

Come, share my world

Feel the emotions of my heart

see the love of my soul

be my voice

isn't it   phenomenal

feel the beat of my heart

see the love of my soul

it is in my blood

come, run away with me

    leave the kids baby

let me give all my best to you.

Let us experience the rhythm of the night

the passion of our voices, our hearts, our souls

your mind.

I have dreamt sweet dreams of this moment

come, run away with me baby.

For I am off the hook behind you

what is wrong? Is my love jones too strong?

ok, I will let it evolve

I can wait, I can be   faithful

forever fate-full

there will be no secret loves or boys on the side,

you know it is our destiny to be together

lets be together

be careful because it is rumored

that I am one of those deadly sins... and then some.

But come

experience my Pure Love

all 100% of it.

Give me another night

Just one night

better than the first

just another night baby.

This time, in the Light

we will not keep it secret

in the morning, in the light

you with your crust on your mouth

"cat-shit" in your eyes

and dog like breath,

I will kiss you

deeply and deeper

and then I will hum.

Hummin' baby.

Returning to a love

Please baby, let me give you something to remember

come home again

home to me

I promise not to leave you again

wet, and soaked

you will not be alone,

> *not again.*

Come, let me end your innocence

opps, I already have!

Give me one more chance

you love me

you must love me

as my brother

through our fraternal brotherhood

give me one more chance

you got me SPELLBOUND

> *SPELLBOUND baby*

why am I so high

> *so high on your words*

why am I missing you?

me, missing you

Me? missing you?

Me?

Missing   you?

Hell yeah baby boy

I am in the Prime of my life

Soon reality will sit in

and I do no want to be lonely tonight

*   not tonight*

not again,   tonight baby?

come back, share my love

come to me baby

Many would marvel at our sight as your COMET would one day progress to a level of that of the SUN. Like my father's father, Hyperion, and my father Helios, I would mount you on my chariot and ride you all day. I would carry you across the sky for all the world to see. You following my lead. Me treating you with love and care; tending to your every need, whim, whimper, desire, and moan. Gasping at the brilliance of your light and radiance. Our chests heaving with the hot air of feeling our lungs expanded from exhaustion while you are BURNING and BURSTING with light and energy. So untouchable and MAGNIFICENT.

On my chariot I will carry you all over the world. Letting others bask in your beauty and brilliance. Me, me. Whipping the massive powerful studs that will carry you. The ones that you so willing mounted at your disposal to carry you for hours. On and on... As you would set ... and I come ... to a halt, in time for your rest, I would return you to our bed and "rest" with you to feel your brilliance and lush beauty in my private and personal channels. In ways, that I wish that only I can experience. Sleeping deeply, I would tend to you, lovingly, affectionately, and tenderly. Never sleeping but rejoicing for my adventurous fortune. Only to get it up again when dawn leaves the stream of the ocean and makes her way up to the sky. Me fashioned in a precious cup and you in your radiant morning beauty, your beauty touching the clouds and shining smiles on our faces, smiles of joy, looks of lust, thoughts to impure in nature to describe the joy that you give unto me. Give ... it... unto me. Again, I would prepare for you and the mounting as the minutes are precious. The feelings of benevolent emotion in abundance to the feelings that would be shown to you. Now radiating from me, for you, consuming you, engulfing you. None other would compare to us, SOL would have *nothing* on us. Then, again, I would mount you ... on my chariot.

After

The day, the night, the noon day, the morning, after,

those days after

I will hold you, caress you, love you, cherish you, after,

those days after

those sweet affectionate days after

reading to you, dancing with you, tripping after you

those days after

Meadow brooks, streams, stars lit, flames roaring and ignite, after

that night, of pure attention

after

after the hurt, the removal of the pain,

The whorish sessions halts,

afterwards

you cause me to run a gambit of emotions

tired, lonely nights,

feelings of depression

thoughts of suicide

feelings of anxiety

confused and dazed

bewilderment, perplexed thoughts

we run a gambit of emotions, after

feelings of stress

dementia

dizziness

paranoia

we run the gambit of emotions,

thoughts to intense to cope with

after,

thoughts that hurt, we look for relief and comfort after

those days after

Chance Encounter

winds blow

pheromones released

a lover arrives

a desire of want

quick knowing looks

eyes aflutter

passion of a touch

a kiss exchanged

pecks on the cheek

a touch of the lips

soft caresses

tongues dueling

heavy breathing

turns taken

a need fulfilled

sublime bliss

Monsieur,

Grasping for words to do unto you such beauty I can not, for descriptions pale such a man of your person. For with this letter I have noth to entreat my sanity of your presence but the memory of your enchanting words. For, my love, with the coming days my desire to see you is unwavered as my heart beat persist. Your letter was received with the fondest of pleasure and delight. Lets make our next meeting as blissful and passionate as our hearts and souls will sustain. Least ye collapse from exhaustion from the brush of a palm to thy cheek, a touch of such a nature shall serve as gratification to my soul, `til eternities end.

Saintly yours,

Yancy.

Dear love,

The hand of a lover has now gone. Missed.

The desire to feel one seems so distant and cold. The flames from my desire now burn furious. The heat of passion's embers begin to spark and kiss my flesh.

Since his departure, his memory begins to wear, my love begins to wain. I keep his memory close.

Now they begin to fade.

The fire fueled on love is not running low.

I feel the presence of a new love.

However, I have nothing to give.

Hopeful,

Desire

A moonlight walk on a dark dusty trail

things pass by

but we trode on

never wondering where

things will go

you seem calm, able to relax

me more tense, wondering if I fit.

I feel its a long shot,

you say it's not.

We reach the pond,

no snakes, little frogs

we hear barks from dogs.

I hold your hand and pull you close

place my hand on your throat

kiss you like before

only without tongue

I know you are afraid, but don't run

I look into your eyes hold you near,

it would last

if you get over your fear.

You seem vulnerable

I seem hurt,

I put that out my mind

and tickle you until it hurts.

I take you home now relax and talk

the sun comes up

it was just dark

we continue to talk

time comes for you to go

with an understanding

that you will come again

through the door.

I need to feel her.

Her curves

her moves

her body.

Hands running over her torso

I need to see her tonight.

be near her

tonight.

in her.

this night.

on her.

all night.

with her

only when it is right.

She does see me.

never knowing me

never experiencing

me.

she's giving

never wanting needing

possessing

but not owning

me.

I give myself to her

more at night sometimes in the day

she is between my legs now,

exposed open,

wanting me inside her, I c-can't resist.

It is inevitable

she is

seductive.

validating

me.

caressing

me.

making me feel like that man that I should be and

giving me what I need

only not as powerful

as I

need

it.

She is seducing

me

and I am seducing her

as we are feeding off each other.

I feel her on my back

caressing me

scratching me

pressing and squeezing

me

pulling all of it

from

me.

I touch her	there
feel her	there
we can't anymore	
I must be	there
she wants it	there
we totally exposed now.	essentially bare
rough rugged and raw we get	there
she first then me	

I had her

tonight.

you leave

feelings hurt

torn shirt

hands hurt

don't do it

desires and intentions

not knowing

you only wanted

this can't be

go on?

you took it and ran.

played yourself

your heart was open

he crushed it

thoughts

feelings hurt

not taking time

remove yourself

healed yourself

hot and steaming

not acheiving

again mistreated.

your defeated

its deceiving

constant misreading

he in your head

him in bed.

you can't see

we can't be.

in his hands

like a lamb

without a glance

provoked

you advance

for romance

from his glance

no romance

stand up

be hers

met a man

closed your heart

hear his tone

took a chance

her only man

didn't want his pants

to romance

take his hand

Letter 5

the sun is hot

the weather calm

breeze blowing

on my neck

on my ears

sweaty hands

dirty palms

sun caressing

my body

sweat trailing on my

lips, thighs, hips

down and over my back

drenching me

basking in a thoughtful dry day

a cool breeze dry me

you dash me with water

its cool makes me smile

the day goes on

nights become warm

I need to feel your arms.

in a crowded room yet totally alone

heart open feelings unknown

not being in love only going through the motions

walking on land yet drowning in the ocean

living life not to the fullest

being on the top of the world yet empty inside

going out to clubs and losing your pride

doing what we do cause that all we know

understanding the difference between a husband and a hoe

cherishing what you have yet looking for more

going from day to day yet still unsure of what's yet to come.

Letter 7

Touching you

rubbing you

licking on your neck.

down your back

to your waist.

placing your hands on my head

...

kissing you

lower

licking on you

slower

turning you

around to the bed

biting you

licking you

slower

parting you

touching you

grabbing you

diggin'

music playing in the background

my hand on your waist

removing your pants

placing my hand on your face

biting you to ignite a spark

feeling on your breast

pressing that

spot

tickling your feet

can i get you in bed?

not for sex

just for talk

i am

more comfortable

that way

Chillin with friends

Ballin in the park

Weights at home in the garage

Gym only by myself

Mall to pick up fits

Suits to show my style

Rims on the car to bump the sound

My Timbs on my favorite limbs

Clubbin to release the stress

Stopping and coming back to reality

I relish

in the thought of him

his scent

his feel

his touch.

He was

is

will always be

sensual.

Easy going

affectionate

I will always be

caring

concerned

attentive

friendly

lively.

Thoughts of him

will never be

strange

withdrawn

emotionless

or daring.

He will be ...

I would be.

I get lost

in thoughts of

him.

About

him.

When talking to

him.

Reality ceases

time stops

and moves on.

Minutes become hours

instantly.

I become more when

I talk with him.

I feel

exist

open up

and simply talking

he ignites that

in me.

Hence,

I relish

thoughts of

him.

It being brand new

I didn't want to hurt

it

use it

lose it

It being mine and new

I had to

explore

it

comfort it

console it

and enjoy

it.

it being different

made it

unusual

nice

carefree

me.

It being mine

I had to

give it away

before I

lose

it.

At times I wonder what I am supposed to say to you.

Today is one of those days. I have gotten to the
point where I feel that I can share with you, and say,
and talk about anything with you. However, right now,
I am at a loss for words.

Today I thought of you for a brief second. Only that
second lasted longer than a minute and then that
minute resulted in a 45 minute call. Just to hear your voice.

I gazed into thin air for about a minute and thought
of you. I could not stop myself from looking at
your picture and seeing your cute ears, beautiful
lips, and soft eyes. I don't know what you see, but I
know what I see. For some reason, I wanted to kiss
you. It was a crazy uncontrollable urge that I could
not help.

I have these feelings for you. You weren't suppose to know. You were supposed to be a friend, only, more. We are getting to know each other. Pals, Friends. Bois. Gym rats even, and at times. More. I would hang out with you and we would do things together. Movies. Converse. Dinner at Applebees. Whatevah. Whatevah you wanted, whenevah you wanted. As long as I was with you. Sadly, we haven't even met or got to the first date.

You would be nice and I would be funny. We would be ourselves. You: brown skin, sensitive, guarded, intelligent, friendly, and seemingly romantic. A dream of anyone's imagination, and everyone's desires. Only, while we were together, I would have you to myself. What many would see from the surface was not what it seems. You have these dark smoldering eyes, which has a sensual softness and calming nature about yourself. Tranquility. Beautiful lips, that I could kiss and kiss, and kiss again.

I want you.

Only I am afraid to tell you. You would leave me if I
did. I know it. You know it. I am taking a risk now, even
thinking about you. Writing about it and saving it as
an email that you may never see. Never read,
only cause of the closeness. It matters to me and
you. I would hold my feelings to myself, and not tell
you. Only, I would wait, to see if you ever say
anything.

At times, I think of you and I think I know what you
are thinking. I think I know what you are feeling. I
am feeling the same. Your voice, words, and tone give
you away. Me too! You come off as concerned. I like
that. With you, I think of the day. The morning and
the night. You come to mind at each time. Your voice
is the first thing I hear in the morning and the last
thing I want to hear at night.

I have thoughts of you. Romantic thoughts. Me holding

you, standing, hand on your waist, pulled close to me. The other hand on your face. Caressing you. I would kiss you on your eyes, your nose, your jaw. The lips. Bite on the chin. Nibble on the ear and neck. Then the lips again, and again, and again.

I had these thoughts and I don't know why. I have a feeling that you have them too. I know it is not just me. Your conversation is pulling me. Engaging. You make me laugh, excited, happy. You can analyze me and be dead on. I want to give you everything, anything, and leave nothing for myself. I want to please you and never stop pleasing you.

Close all the shades

lock all the doors

Today this minute I feel

numb.

Block out the sun

turn off the fun

Don't let your emotions take hold

and run.

Don't take over the moment

Allow it to be

Wonder how far this will go

Just you wait and see.

Smooth and charming as always

be yourself and see

only don't get caught out there

exposing yourself for free.

This moment now I feel

nothing

Yet in time I feel

something.

Woke by the phone

hear his voice and smile

he is talking about sex again

this is pulling me down.

I remain open and cheerful

to hear his voice once more

I wonder how he came to this choice

of words not like before.

He makes it clear what he wants

I don't respond

I only know it will only come

in its own time.

He is asking my feelings now

and I don't have any at all

I am trying to stop a runaway horse

before he trips and falls.

I try to be funny

back to my normal self

It now occurs to me

to put my emotions on the shelf.

Letter 13

I was supposed to write one message.

I wrote two.

I kept one to myself.

The other I sent to you.

You seem to be nice

and that seems to be true.

I hope you are this way

and theirs nothing funny about you.

For some reason you feel nervous

and with that I understand.

During tonight's events

I may only shake your hand.

I am not pulling away

I am remaining calm and true.

One thing is for sure

I will not be caught out there fallin over you.

I have to guard my feelings

and not let them show.

Things may change in the future

and I will never know.

I have to be honest with myself

I want to make sure.

That no one is treated

like the common whore.

We will keep it real and simple

I will be open and true.

I hope you will be yourself

and not someone other than you.

In this day

in this hour

I know not

by what power

i don't know

i can't see

how this dude

would even fall for me.

he seems nice

i do care

i know one thing

he must keep on his underwear

i want to open up

relax and even share

but i really wonder

if this brotha even care.

the conversations were nice

and i really began to share

this brotha does not know me

and yet he still wants to go there.

he admits to having feelings

something i must have caused

i sent him poems while he was away

and everyday i called.

he is a nice brotha

that i can not lie.

however i know about my emotions

hence i will not lie.

i will be open to share

and see where this will actually go.

but i know for sure one thing

i will not treat him like the common hoe.

i know not how this will play out

i can not give that a thought.

i know that he will win out

hence emotions and feelings are for naught.

You have to stop this broh.

Thanks for saying that my writing is a blessing. I received this email after I said that I would not send you any more poems and such. Well, I will have to think about that. In my own head and in my own time, I will have to come to my own decision of whether I will share them with you or not.

I am willing to share with you. However, have no misconceptions. I will always share with you. When I am ready, I will share more and not less. I am happy you are blessed by the poems and I am happy for you. In time, they may come again. I will continue to write them, but I have to decide if I will share them.

Now, on a different note.

I still want you. Now only as a friend, but I have to

let you know this.   We could be passionate lovers,
and we could be damn good friends. I would hate to
have the way you act be a factor in destroying that.
Really I would. I think you are a nice person, and to
answer your question about why you stay with your wife
and who would want you.

Honestly, I can not say you will or can do better. I
know not that. I do know that I would have accepted a
man with three kids, or five for that matter, into my
life and home without a batting of an eye and without
a thought of the consequences, if he was a damn good
friend and a passionate lover.

I always believe you can have both, but sometimes one
will win out over the other.   "Fear nothing not even
your true self or your emotions" is how I live my
life. However you are just existing.

Letter 16

I needed to see him

feel his warmth

love his smile

meet his friends

experience his world

bash in his arms

know more about him

I took a chance

on a simple glance

he was what I wanted

I am what he needed

we complimented each other

it should be

we could be

i must be

only he knows the truth

that we will not be

I could not give him anything. I had nothing left to give. He had taken everything and left me with nothing but the memories and the essence of what we were.

It was not something that I would have changed, or anything that I would have done differently. For me the memories alone were wonderful; the experience exciting; the thoughts and potential endless. However, that was not the case anymore. He took everything from me and left me with nothing!

I liked it that way, it gave me a chance to replenish. I knew that things would return, the feeling, the emotion, the surrendering, the outpour of facts, acts, deeds, and desire. I would not hold that against him for taking what he needed.

I would not hold it against him for being what he was:

desirable and endearing.

I could not help it.

He had his needs and I had my desires. We were to be
what we were, and nothing more than that.

Lovers.

He would have what he needed and I would have what I
wanted. Here is how it occurred:

He kissed me and I kissed him back. It was the scent
of his essence. His lips, his hands, his eyes, the
roughness of his cheeks and the curve of his lips.
I pulled him closer, he looked into my eyes. I could
not resist. I did not want to. We nuzzled and I could
not stand it anymore. I needed to be with him and
could not wait any longer.

I placed my hand on his face, caressed his cheeks and

began to play with his ears.

He smiled.

I tickled his ears, behind them and moved in for the kill. ... I had to have them in my mouth and tug on them with my teeth.

You are in my world. I felt him. I became extremely emotional with imaginative actions that went against my thoughts.

I kissed him. ... On his neck, his ears, and with my teeth, I pulled slightly at them. He moaned, I kissed harder.

He tried to pull away, I went with him.

He asked me to stop. I could not continue? I wanted him and I wanted him to know it. I looked at him as he began to remove his shirt. I stopped him.

I could not have this occur like this, not here, in this place. We wanted to get exposed in this place, this house, in this way.

I could not have it, I wanted him yes, he wanted me, but it would not happen here on the bed, in his bedroom. It was to ... intimate. To loving, to knowing, to lasting.

We needed it to be different, freakier, strange, but exciting. I needed to be with him on the bathroom floor ... or on the couch, or the stairs.

I would not have it any other way.

He tried to take off his shirt, I would not allow it.

I took him by the hand, led him to the stairs and turned around. He wondering where were we going, and I said, we are there. He was not surprised, only he wanted it to happen there too. I turned him around, and ripped his shirt.

I would pay for this one, like the others.

I had to rip it from him. It was keeping me from him! What could I do? I had no choice. I could not have that.

We were into this and he was feeling it ... I needed to feel him. I sat on the stairs and he began to open his legs. I stood between them and started to remove his pants. This was not unusual, but he wanted me to do it with teeth... only not as rough as last time. I tend to get rough at times. I did not mind, as long as he did not alert the neighbors as before.

Letter 18

Let go my love.

It was not there any more.

It could not exist.

It was not meant to be.

We tried and it failed.

I could hear your wails at night

as you

let go of

my love.

It was the moon

stars

the earth

sun

the wind

his breathe

our feelings

the thoughts

a burning sense of compassion

his faith

my desire

her belief

a sense of connection

no remorse

we would have it

he would never need it

he had a lost

i had a desire

we had nothing beyond tonight.

remove the stars from the sky

place them in a basket

let no one have them.

stop the flowers from blooming

place them someplace cold.

blot out the sun.

replace it with a starless night

bring the moon in closer.

bigger and brighter.

now dull it.

look into his eyes.

place the liberated stars in them.

look at his smile.

see how he makes picked flowers bloom.

the world is brighter.

even without the sun.

he smiles, my heart warms, and

the universe is right

even when it is disfigured.

The Epitome of a Man?

...

we sat on the floor,

listening to soft music, holding each other,

you leaning on my chest

me with one arm around your waist

the other playing in your hair.

I turn down the lights

walk across the room

and

light the candle

scented,

alluring,

we embrace

our eyes

focus

we embrace

our hands,

wander

we

embrace

it.

I draw you closer

in my heart

we get to know each other

calmer now

relaxed

transfixed to the thoughts that make us known.

You place your head back on my chest

I cross my legs under your back

to let you become

comfortable.

I place my hand on your thigh

you listen to my heart beat

I feel your pulse.

We communicate

The music washes over us

we

grow closer...

My mind wanders

the music stops

Our music begins

I kiss you

deeply,

passion,

touches

I whisper into your ear

you

respond

I kiss it

you

moan

we

respond

you

relax

The candle burns

the scent,

alluring

I caress you

our hearts, link

WE moan

holding your face, I look into your eyes

...

I position myself above you.

I look into your eyes they are

vivid,

dancing,

inviting,

vulnerable.

I kiss you on the eyes -peckingly

your cheeks -softly

your lips -awkwardly

Control.

Keep Control!

Don't rush!

I look into you.

Your heart

it beats, it blooms

WE blossom.

I unbutton your shirt

push it back over your shoulders

unresisting, now

you open your heart

unresisting,

NOW

I run my fingers over your chest

feeling you quiver, feel the beat, the pulse -quickening

vulnerable

I remove my shirt

vulnerable

I place my hands on your chest

rubbing you,

caressing you,

relax baby.

I move to your face

hold your cheeks in the palm of my hand,

right there

baby.

I place my fingers on your shoulders

lower

i trace fingernail markers on your chest

so sorry baby

I whisper into your ear,

"don't worry, everything will be all right..."

I remove your pants,

mine now

I get the lotion

VASELINE Brand INTENSIVE CARE

16 FL. OZ - 3 now

Blue bottle

SNAP shut top

Patent No.

4,939,179 & D318,423

irrelevant

insatiable

I lean over you

I look at you

survey your body,

inspect the goods that

are now,

mine,

YES MINE.

The looks

the chest

the torso

hips, thighs, feet, heart, emotions

passion

I inspect THE goods

...

I turn you over

place the lotion into my hands,

warm it,

NICE

Rub it in, deeper, smoother,

down your back

"How do you want your massage?"

"Mmm....that's fine....mmm."

i apply pressure

on the shoulder -more lotion,

on the back -more lotion

over the waist -less lotion

further down - DON'T touch THERE -   (not now...)

Control.

Keep Control!

Don't rush.

Over the hips -less lotion

down the thighs -more lotion

around the calves

on the feet

through the toes

again

more pressure

more pleasurable

slower now.

i turn you over

now the front

full body massage baby

the chest

the stomach

the abdomen

arms

lower

the hips

shin

feet

once again baby,

once again.

Control.

Keep...

....

You are on me

vulnerable

i see the candle again

burning

scented,

alluring.

You turn me over, lotion your hands,

I think

'Oh, God' - "mmph!"

over the back -less lotion

over the waist -less lotion

on the buttocks -More lotion

you rub it in deeper,

harder,

smoother,

again

massage

kneeled

...

insert

pain

relax baby, relax

teeth biting lips

pain

"mmph."

pushing - "mmph."

probing - "mmph."

deeper - "mmph."

faster - "MMPH."

"SSSHHHHHH..."

i am

silenced

rocking

wanting

needing

faster

...

"ready...?"

i respond

You recede

We embrace

i pull you down on me

we kiss

i see a candle in your eyes, lit from a spark unknown

burn candle,

burn

we kiss

it burns.

...

You prepare - i wait

thinking

'Oh God!!! i... i'

we sit

up

we prepare - i am ready

straddle

"Mmph."

lower

"Lie back"

'Oh God!!. i... i'

"Relax."

'Oh, God!.. i... i   please, please, ... pleasure.'

i look into your eyes

i see the light from a candle

burn candle,

burn.

Our hearts link

we moan

i run my fingers over you back

beads of sweat, and lotion

panting,

deeper,

thrust,

deeper,

thrusting,

Pumping

Pumping

Pumping

thoughts, emotions, words, -mix

i look into your eyes

see a light

burn candle

'Bern"

Pumping

                                        Pumping

Pumping

Intimacy

He touched my body from behind

hands around my waist

lips and tongue at my ear...

my hands cover his fingers

intertwined.

I guide them along my waist to my thighs.

Why am I gay, I wonder.

I turn around

he lifts me to the counter

we kiss

hands roving

tongues dueling

legs spread

his hand on my butt,

the other on the back of my head pushin' my head towards his.

I grab the back of his head

run my fingers through his hair

and he sucks my tongue deeper into his mouth.

The suction is so intense and strong,

the underside of my tongue is bruised

from my teeth and the prolong stretching.

Gosh that feels good.

Twenty minutes of passionate kissing

we break

breath.

My hands rove his body:

chest, nipples, arms, neck, face

caress his face and hold his jaw lovingly.

He is sweet, so giving, a keeper. I won't play this one.

I take his hand and lead him to the bedroom

dark

but cool.

I sit him down

remove his shoes

and push him down on his back.

Passive-aggressive tendencies tend to surface during moments of

intense

pleasure.

"Bossy bottoms" --NOT!

Straddle him.

Unbutton his shirt and fell his chest and nipples.

Roll them between my fingers

hear him wench from the pain

see him squirm from the pleasure.

Fell his hands on my butt.

Caress them cheeks baby.

Bend down and kiss him face

eyes and lips.

He is so sweet.

Deep passionate kissing.

Hands tuggin' at zippers

pants pulled off

bare cheeks exposed,

and pulled apart.

Crevices explored with finger tips.

Damn baby, I like it like that, ruff.

We embrace. Lets slow down baby.

Touching now.

Fingers pressing, poking, proding, rubbing,

nipples, lips, eyes, jaw, stomach, waist, penis, thighs,

thick, strong, sensual, romantic, freaky.

I kiss him and pull his body to mine.

His hands rub down my back.

He kisses his way to my jaw bone and bites it,

downward he travels

slowly licking my neck

now he bites.

Oh! Stop damn it!

Don't! Stop!

Don't .... stop! Damn it!

Dont stop damn it.

Ummm....yess like that baby.

Don't stop damn it.

Don't stop! Ummm...

One hand rubs his head

and push his face into my neck.

The fingers of my other hand dig into his back muscles.

His fingernails dig into my butt cheeks

pulling them

squeezing them

kneeding them.....

that's right

ruff baby, ruff.

I lock my legs under his thighs and roll him on top of me.

I kiss his nipples

suck on the left, pinch the right.

He is in a semi-push-up stance, sweating.

I suck harder

bite

lick

blow cool air on them

bite harder

pull on those big erasers.

Tug harder.

I *know* he likes that. He/We into that kinky shit.

He screams, and falls on top of me.

Un-un!

I slap that bare ass!

"Get back on those hands!"

He obeys.

"Damn baby you gettin' me hot."

"I am just gettin' to know your body," I state.

I continue sucking
he sweats more.
It drips from his body down my face,
from his thighs to my hips.
He screams and moans.

He rolls off of me on his side.

"What's wrong baby?"

"Nothing...it's just too intense."
I place my dick between his butt cheeks,
and I start a slow circular grinding motion with my hips.
He joins me.

Our legs intertwine,

his hand pushes my body in closer to his as he pushes back.

I kiss his neck

suck on his ear lobe

and push my tongue into his ear.

I grab his butt.

"Can I get some of this?"

"Only if I can get some of this."

He grabs my dick.

"Naw baby, I don't want to give up some tonight, I am tired.

I am going to sleep."

"Oh no you don't!

You don't get me heated and then go to sleep.

You better WAKE THE FUCK UP and give up that dick!"

Explicit Intimacy

Kissing him felt different.
It was ... relaxing.
I had never kissed him like this
and it made me want to kiss him more.
I placed my hands on his face and caressed
his cheeks.

His tongue was nice and it felt good in my mouth.

He has always felt good in my mouth.

I kissed him
deeper
and moved my hands down his face,
across his chest,
and towards the buttons on his shirt.

I liked the way he felt,
so I felt him.

I unbuttoned the buttons on his shirt, and
removed it. He did not stop me,
and he did not want me to stop.
I never stop--unless asked, but that has never
happened.

He removed
my pull over shirt and we let it fall to the floor.
He kissed me
on my neck and I bit him on his.
I can be a vampire, but I know he loves it...
rough.

I pulled on his nipples,
and kissed him deeper like the first time.
He loved the way that I rolled my tongue
around his and then took his
tongue into my mouth.
The last time I bruised it.
He ran his fingers
down my back and across my butt.

I broke the kiss, stopped the
tugging of the nipples and
began to remove his pants.

He did not resist.

I undressed him and
pulled up a chair behind him.

The wooden one.
I didn't want it to get sticky.
I wanted him to sit on the
chair this time.

Standing between his legs, I removed
my pants and he touched my chest
while I undressed in front of him.
He liked it when I put myself on
display for him.
He kissed my waist
I cradled his head in my hands and
rubbed my fingers through his hair.

He licked and bit on my nipples.
I didn't remove his face from my chest.

His teeth were rougher, but I liked
it.

I removed the Butter Pecan ice cream
and the spoon from the frig and placed it
between his legs.

He flinched from the cold.

I positioned myself between his legs
while he sat on the chair and I
kissed him on his neck.

He liked the way that it felt and his legs
began to shake from the cold container.

I liked the way that he shook.

I kissed my way downward...
over the chest,
around his nipples,
down his stomach and
around his waist.
Stopping at his pubic hairs, and yes ...
I licked them too.

I got the spoon already and I opened the container of
ice
cream.

He looked at me with his puppy dog eyes
and I looked back
at him with
love and adoration.

The ice cream was more of a liquid now.

I liked it in liquid form.

He opened his legs and let me begin my
descend.

I placed the spoon in the liquid and
I feed him a scoop with nuts.

Some spilled on his nipple.
That would be his last spoonful.
I would eat
the rest.

I licked it off his nipple and
he grabbed my head.
I removed
his hands
from my head and
I continued to lick his nipples.
He moaned.

I placed more on the spoon and
I made a trail from his neck to his right
shoulder and I began to lick it up.

He moaned ... I licked.

I licked and bit his neck,
and then his shoulder.
He moaned.
I placed more ice cream on him.
Now on the ear and some
on his chest.

He did not like the cold spoon, but I did.

We liked the flow,
the movement,
the energy.

I licked his ear,
and I dove my tongue into his
ear.

Licking the insides,
and then the lobe.

Biting it, blowing cool air on
it.
Tonguing behind
it.

He grabbed my head again, I removed his hands.

He moaned and groaned.

I liked the sounds he made.

He could not take the cold of the ice cream,
and he began to move and stir in the chair.

I liked
it.
Seeing him stirring.

I licked over his chest, and removed the ice cream, but he was not
done
yet.

I had a pint of ice cream and all night.
(I haven't even touched his back ...
yet.)
I spread his legs wider and I moved closer between them.
I placed
more ice
cream
on his nipples, and I trailed it too his waist. He moaned
and
I licked.
I place it on his stomach, and his thighs.
This time with
nuts.

I chewed on his thighs and then his stomach.
I placed it on his dick. He jumped,
and fell on the floor.
I helped him back to the chair and he liked
the flow.
He begged me to hold up. I could not,
I had lots of ice cream
left.

I liked the way he felt in my mouth.

I placed more ice cream on his dick.
And I licked it off.
First the head,
then the shaft.
I pulled the foreskin of his dick up and over the head. I
placed ice cream inside the hole made by his foreskin.
He stirred more in the chair.
He could not take the coldness of the ice cream.
Butter Pecan, baby.

I pulled down on the shaft and let the liquid flow.
I deep throated
his dick to catch all the liquid before it hit his balls.
Damn baby, lets do
that
again.
So I did.
We did.
I did.
We did.

I placed more ice cream on his thighs, with nuts.
I chewed on his thighs
and he liked the way my tongue felt.

I poured some ice cream on his chest,
I heard him "whew," "ewhh," and moan.
I chewed, I licked, and I moaned.
He looked down into my eyes.
I placed ice cream on his balls. He jumped.
I held him down this time.
I licked it and tongued his balls.
Rolling them
in my mouth
licking
them.
He liked the way that my tongue felt.
I liked the way that his balls tasted.
How I missed that.

I poured ice cream on the small area in his public hairs
between his dick and his thighs.
I placed his legs over my shoulders,
hands behind his back,
and I began to lick and bite.

Baby jumped, and baby moaned,
but baby wasn't going anywhere.
I dove in further
licked harder, and bit harder.
Baby, moaned
louder.

I placed more ice cream over his dick,
and I deep throated it again.
Damn he felt
good.

I held his right leg up and placed more ice
cream
on the back of his knee.
I licked and I bite.
He jumped and moaned.
I held tighter on his leg.
One down, one more to go.

I released him.

Time for the back.
I asked him to turn around in the chair
and place his butt a little off the edge of the seat.
He complied.
I liked
the way his butt looked on the edge of the chair.
So round, and big.
I sat
in the chair with him.
He on my thighs and our legs spread. Both of us
backwards.

I placed more ice cream on his ears

and I licked it off.

He moaned
more
and I licked
more.

I pulled on his nipples and I licked the ice cream from
the other ear.
My dick between his legs,
and his back to my chest.

I removed myself from the chair.
His butt still on the edge.
I placed more ice cream
on
him.
On his back. I trailed it from his shoulder
to his mid back.
I licked
sucked
and bit him.

He moaned,
and groaned,
and flinched.
I licked from his shoulders to his waist to remove
all the ice
cream.
He liked the feel.

I pulled his butt cheeks apart
and I poured ice cream between his cheeks.
He jumped.
I tongued his butt.

First the outside on the cheeks, then the
inside along the crack.
I licked
and I licked.

I poured more ice cream on his butt.
Directly on the hole.
I dove in and I licked.
Moving my tongue in
and out, and around in circles
while pulling the cheeks apart.
Baby, loved
it.

I loved it too
baby.

I loved it, too.
Baby.

I poured more ice cream on his back.
At the small of his back
and I let it run down between his butt cheeks.
I met it with my tongue at the base of
his butt.
I let it drip onto my tongue.
I savored the tasted and I licked
it up and
I licked over him.
I cleaned him and then
I licked him all over.
He liked the feel.

I wasn't done yet!
Not yet.

I still had the nuts and a little more ice cream left.
I placed the nuts into my mouth.
I used my tongue to place them at the
opening of his butt and I pushed one into
him.
He jumped and I licked.
I pushed another,
and another,
and them some more into him.
He jumped
and I licked.

And then I chewed and ate them from him.

I poured the last of the ice cream
from his butt to his dick.
I licked my
way back
to his dick.
I liked the way it felt.
I turned him in his chair,
and I continued to suck his dick.

I liked the way he felt in my mouth.